T0196945

The ELEUTHERIAN
VOYAGERS *and*
BEYOND

The ELEUTHERIAN VOYAGERS *and* BEYOND

A GENEALOGICAL STUDY OF EARLY ELEUTHERANS

GABRIELLE F. CULMER

THE ELEUTHERIAN VOYAGERS AND BEYOND
A GENEALOGICAL STUDY OF EARLY ELEUTHERANS

iUniverse books may be ordered through booksellers or by contacting:

iUniverse
1663 Liberty Drive
Bloomington, IN 47403
www.iuniverse.com
1-800-Authors (1-800-288-4677)

Because of the dynamic nature of the Internet, any web addresses or links contained in this book may have changed since publication and may no longer be valid. The views expressed in this work are solely those of the author and do not necessarily reflect the views of the publisher, and the publisher hereby disclaims any responsibility for them.

Any people depicted in stock imagery provided by Getty Images are models, and such images are being used for illustrative purposes only. Certain stock imagery © Getty Images.

ISBN: 978-1-5320-5442-6 (sc)
ISBN: 978-1-5320-5443-3 (e)

Library of Congress Control Number: 2018908550

Print information available on the last page.

iUniverse rev. date: 08/15/2018

Special thanks to G. Clifford, my father, for the patience and support of this project, and to my aunts and uncles, who provided encouragement. Also, thank you to the sources and resources used in compiling the project.

INTRODUCTION

I have compiled many years of research into this project to detail the study of the first settlers to the Bahamas. I initially gained an interest while doing a vast genealogical study of my background and how part of my family came to be on the medium-sized island of Eleuthera. History has always been a favourite topic of mine, and I have researched public sources to compile this information, some of which I have been familiar with for the last thirty years through my study of European, Bahamian, and US history in high school. I have been compelled to publish as resources have grown scarcer and family members are maturing.

The study begins with the history of some of the families and then details the lives of their descendants who are related and not related through various reasons. It is difficult to claim a common ancestry without an expert. However, one can focus on the similarities in their struggles in different locations. Although proud to be a modern-day member of these families, I also commend many other people with similar plights who have travelled and had to build either nations or institutions. Many innovative people have come from Eleuthera. This book will assist those who wish to research their family trees with similar ties to the process and my journey.

It is inspiring how a select group built a nation while, in modern times, others build nations and businesses. Regardless of the personalities of the forefathers, whether they were considered flawed or secular, they faced many difficulties. For example, in the late 1800s on Eleuthera, two heads of the same family were wiped out by dysentery in the same year. Women birthed children at home and did not survive. Other settlers were stressed when crops refused to grow. These problems are comparable to issues faced in modern times.

This book serves to provide the reader with an understanding of the journey of several families to the new world and to offer a glimpse into their own ancestry. It can be appreciated by all with a keen interest in history and family research. I found myself in an easier position to understand and access family research through my love of history and travels to Eleuthera. I have always felt the need to give back to a community that has given so much to me and helped to instil in me values of altruism.

This is the history of Eleuthera and how many people from the islands came to be.

CHAPTER 1

Early Sands History

It is disputed from where exactly the Sands family originated and from whom they are descended. Research has suggested that there is barely a common basis among migrants who arrived in the nineteenth century on the great wave from Europe. However, one prong of the surname (via Edwyn Sandys) and its derivatives are famous throughout history and may be remotely connected to the others in many ways as visionaries. Their initial strategic planning may have assisted in the growth and migration of many to follow. The Sands, Sandys, or Sondes families have formed worldwide a strong lineage throughout history.

The name, Sandys or Sands, is meant to have stemmed from Norman Vikings who conquered Western Europe. It is from the place in England where they settled near Burgh on Sandes in Cumberland, with the registration of Simon de Sandis or Sablums in the year 1234, when

Simon de Sandis (Sabulanibus) granted a plot of land.[1] The Bretons continued to Normandy, from where they were said to have arrived, with William the Conqueror in 1066, and formed a base in Northern England.[2] In St Bees Lancashire, there is a registration for Robert Del Sandes, where the family was granted land and a castle in appreciation of their support. They remained here and near Lake Windermere, expanding throughout the War of the Roses until the 1500s. Then they were supported by Henry VII through the Tudor period until the 1600s, when many deviated and migrated to the new world.[3] By this point there were many derivatives of the spelling of their name, perhaps some from a notable line. The Scottish line is said to have started migration from England in the early 1400s and used the name Sands.

The topic, which is courageously depicted of the Vine and Esthwaite prongs (the archbishop Edwyn is also described as connected to and descended from Isabel d'Avenel who was associated with William the Lion of Scotland[4]), has been reserved in an earlier popular tale: They served their country of origin and leaders and were highly respected. My research concentrates, from public documents, and of interest, on a Richard Sands, born 1610 in Lancashire, who was noted as the son of Edwin Sands, born 1561 in England and died 1629 in England. Richard, born circa 1629, married Hester Aucher, who

---

[1] www.sandsancestry.net, p. 1, accessed 24 August 2014.

[2] Pleasants, *The Lovelace Family and Its Connections*, 227–28.

[3] Ibid.

[4] https://en.wikipedia.org/wiki/William_the_Lion.

was born in 1638 and died in Lancashire in 1699. He was the father of Stephen Sands. However, there are other public records to indicate a Peter Sands, born to a Richard and Hester Sands, lived in Kent.[5] During the same period, a record has also been found of a Colonial Richard and Hester Sands living in Somers Isle (Bermuda) in the 1650s and owning property at Hog Bay in Sandys.[6] Also, a Richard Sandys of Downhall Kent, a Parliament colonel, died in 1669, married Hester Aucher, and had six sons and four daughters.[7]

A number of the Sandys or Sandes men were knighted in the fifteenth, sixteenth, and seventeenth centuries— namely, Sir William Sands (Sandall) in 1471; John Saundes in 1487; William Sandes (by Henry VIII) in 1523; Richard Sandes in 1598; Michael Sands or Sondes in 1603; Edwin Sandes of Kent on 28 June 1603; John Sandes of Buckinghamshire in 1608; Myles Sandes of Greenwich in 1621; and Miles Sands of Cambridge in December 1628.[8]

Before changing subjects to concentrate on the voyage, I would like to note that this Sandys family at the time had married into families who were connected to aristocrats. Many of the women were ladies-in-waiting for

---

[5] www.familysearch.org.

[6] Sir John Henry Lefroy, *Memorials of the Discovery and Early Settlement of the Bermudas or Somers Islands, vol. II,* 726.

[7] Pleasants, *The Lovelace Family and Its Connections,* 240.

[8] *The Knights of England: A Complete Record from the Earliest Time to the Knights of Present Day of All the Orders of Chivalry on England, Scotland, and Ireland and of Knights Bachelors,* www.archives.org, last visited 25 August 2014.

two or three monarchs. They also financially supported the reigning king in his restoration, and a few served in his father's parliament. However, further fields awaited some members of the extended family and those with the same surname.

Many travelled back and forth to Virginia, including the poet brother of Sir Edwyn, George Sandys, as well as other relatives to the new world. Others moved to the Kent area, where a Peter Sands was born. He was noted as the son of Richard and Hester. Archbishop Edwyn Sr's half-brother, William, moved to Ireland,[9] capturing a whole other lineage of those who migrated in the 1800s to the United States to escape the Irish famine.

Somers Isle and Eleuthera

Starting in 1635, settlers migrated to Somers Isle, organized by Sir Edwin Sandys, the Earl of Southampton and governor of the Virginia Company.[10] Colonial Richard Sandys was a representative on the island.[11]

Those settlers set sail upon the *Dorset* with William Alburie and Thomas and Margaret Pynder as well as on the *True Love*. Many ships left Somers Isle for the Bahama Islands, including Charlestown and Eleuthera. The details are as follows: *The Rebecca and Anne*, 22 June 1656 for

[9] Pleasants, Ibid.

[10] Lefroy, *Memorials of the Discovery and Early Settlement of the Bermudas or Somers Islands, 699.*

[11] Lefroy, Ibid., 726.

Segatoo (Eleuthera); *The William* for Eleuthera on 24 April 1661; and *The Hope* on 19 December 1661. Further, *The Bermodian's Adventure* set sail on 21 February 1669; *The Supplie* on 15 March 1669; *Endeavour* in June 1670; and *The Gertrude* in 1670.[12] Also, the *Blessing* brought the members of the freed people in Somers Isle along with English puritans to Eleuthera in 1657.[13] These new settlers lived freely on Eleuthera.

Notably, many Sandys or Sands men travelled to Virginia during the early settlement. Ships' records involve George and William Sandys. William Sands died in Virginia in 1624, and the record shows an Alexander Sanders travelling in 1633 upon *The Trittelotie*.[14] The Sands men were highly visionary in their ventures.

Those who migrated faced harsh conditions in the new world. Much later, in the 1800s, the Scottish line to Eleuthera migrated from Fife, Ayrshire, and the Hebrides. Included in the lines of those were William and Alexander, who first appeared in the census from the 1400s in Clackmannan and Renfrew.[15]

---

[12] Ibid., table of contents.

[13] Craton, *A History of the Bahamas* (1987).

[14] H. Charles Sandy, *Dawn to Twilight in American Colonization*; *The Dictionary of National Biography*, vol. XXV.

[15] National Records of Scotland, Births, www.ancestry.com.

CHAPTER 2

The Eleutherian Adventurers' Story

I've been familiar with the story of the Eleutherian Adventurers for several decades, since high school in Nassau, where our history teacher told us that we could be descended from these people—and some of us were. For some, their story has been bittersweet. Many have read about the sacrifices their ancestors made to start a new country. A constitution, written to practice free religion, now hangs in Parliament in Nassau.

The island of Eleuthera seemed remote to the world, but William Sayle Captain decided to provide the expedition for those who wanted to leave Somers Isle for social and economic reasons. A group of seventy settlers set sail in 1648 and were forced to trade ambergris and braziletto. The conditions were harsh, the land unyielding. The laws of the land were still strict and religious. Some settlers returned or moved to Jamaica. It is said that thirty-five determined settlers remained. One source noted, "Peter

Sands sworne, saith he and Mr. Nathaniell Sayle were at Eleuthera together. And there was a paper that had a seale at it, which was published in the Cave, but what the contents of it, he knoweth not."[16] It is then stated that this may have been the Royal Charter.

The remaining people were joined by others over the next decade, and in 1670 the lands were granted to the Lord Proprietors of the Carolinas.[17] These were British lords who now owned the property in Eleuthera. Prior to settling, properties had likely been vacant for about a hundred years.

The settlers also sent a contribution, one of the largest gifts for that period, to the newly founded Harvard College. The connections between the early settlers of the new world were close among the different locations.[18]

Culmers

Around the same time, one part of the Culmer family became popular. According to public record, they were one of the first recorded Culmer families; most had arrived in AD 792 in West Sussex in Thanet. Notably Gurth and Stephen Kulmer, seafaring brothers, were allegedly the sons of a Viking chieftain.[19] The name Kulmer was

---

[16] Robert Lefroy, *Memorials of the Bermudas*, vol. II, 235, 236 in Proceedings of the Massachusetts Historical Society. www.archive.org.

[17] Craton, Ibid., 54–9.

[18] Ibid.

[19] Culmer genealogy, www.familysearch.org.

derived from a small island off the coast of Sweden. There is also speculation that the name derived from *cul mer*, or cool waters, or people who lived in a specific area in England.[20]

Whatever the situation, they maintained a low level of existence for hundreds of years, until the presence of Baron Henry and his son Sir Richard, followed by his son, a priest in Kent. Richard Culmer (born ca. 1597) married Katherine Johnson in the summer of 1624. Their children included Richard, James, Ann, Katherine, and Elizabeth.[21] Another George Culmer investigated the hundreds of years of previous land grants and wills for the family that lived in Broadstairs.[22] They were shipbuilders who contributed to that community for many years.[23] It is unknown how they are linked to the migrating family.

Other Culmers listed include a forefather of Virginia, Thomas Culmer Sr, born circa 1597, who married Judith, born in 1598, in 1611.[24] A Judith Culmer was the mother of Thomas Jr, who was born in 1621 in Yorkshire and died in 1662 in Virginia.[25] (Details of Judith's death are unknown.) Thomas Jr married Eliza Blake, born in England, and had a daughter, Hannah Culmer, later the wife of Nicholas Sessums in Virginia. They had

---

[20] Culmer family crest and history, www.houseofnames.com.

[21] https://en.wikipedia.org/wiki/Richard_Culmer.

[22] History of Broadstairs, https://en.wikipedia.org/wiki/Broadstairs.

[23] Culmer genealogy, 862–1913, www.familysearch.org.

[24] "From the Register of the Parish of St John in Thanet, Kent, Oct 1559 to March 1635"; also see St John's Parish Margate vol. 76, Jan. 1922.

[25] www.familysearch.org.

a difficult start, and Hannah married twice, also to a Lane. (Coincidentally, there is also one Richard Lane who drowned in Eleuthera in the 1650s.[26] This family is listed as original settlers, but it is unknown what their connection is to the branch in Eleuthera.)

From the birth and registrar records, another Thomas Culmer[27] was born in Kent in 1618 in Burchington to Thomas Culmer Sr. Around the same time, a Thomas and Judith Culmer married in Kent circa 1620.[28] However, a Thomas and Judith migrated to Eleuthera along with a Daniel Culmer, who had a wife, Mary, and one son, Thomas.[29]

Eleuthera was meant to be the first republic of the new world,[30] and many people sailed there from Somers Isle. It is noted in the Bahama Islands census that an early settler, Peter Sands, married Sarah Wright.[31]

These people formed a new world under harsh conditions on barren land where they had been shipwrecked off the coast of North Eleuthera in *The Sayle* under the direction of Captain William Sayle. They formed the Preacher's Cave, where thirty-five settlers were able to worship and exist under harsh conditions

[26] Full Text of Virginia County Records 975.5, V6 pt. 1, 1909, www.archives.org.

[27] www.familysearch.org.

[28] Kent Registry Church Records, St John's Parish Margate, vol. 76, Jan. 1922.

[29] Bahama Islands Census Records, 1670–1720.

[30] *A History of the Bahamas*, Proceedings of the Massachusetts Historical Society, www.archive.org.

[31] Bahama Islands Census Records, 1670.

without basic necessities and on the sale of braziletto and ambergris.[32] They were given assistance via a shallop (light sailboat) from Massachusetts. They visited the United States for help but remained in the Eleuthera 1720 census and beyond. Also, in the 1670s, *The Gertrude* arrived from Somers Isle with a second migration of settlers.[33] Many were discouraged, as Eleuthera had been described as an "isle in the middle of the ocean."[34]

Tarpum Bay. Copyright Gabrielle F. Culmer

---

[32] Craton, Ibid.
[33] Lefroy, Ibid.
[34] Ibid.

Central Eleuthera. Copyright Gabrielle F. Culmer

Central Eleuthera. Copyright Gabrielle F. Culmer

Central Eleuthera. Copyright Gabrielle F. Culmer

Northern Eleuthera. Copyright Gabrielle F. Culmer

Northern Eleuthera. Copyright Gabrielle F. Culmer

CHAPTER 3

New Portsmouth (Rock Sound)

I. Sands

In 1723, it was alleged that Peter and Sarah had one son, John Sands. Peter Sands Sr had travelled to Boston to seek help in the early years; however, his pleas were misinterpreted because of the island's involvement in the whaling industry. They were allegedly viewed as competition.[35] It is noted that assistance was granted previously.

By 1734, there came into existence a William Sands from the group and his wife, Martha, while a Sarah Sands was still a single woman at the time. By 1740 Samuel and his wife, Sarah, had William and later Samuel. It is also noted that a John Sands was born in the 1840s in Rock

---

[35] Internet source—Department of Archives/Births Registry, Baptismal records of Eleuthera.

Sound to a Catherine Ann.[36] These individuals were noted as having been registered in the census for that time period and my research does not go further. There are listings of another Peter Sands Jr and Sr with families, who lived in the nineteenth century on Eleuthera. Both died in the late 1870s of dysentery.[37] It is unknown how they are related to the original adventurer Sands family, but they lived in the same area; however, it is likely evidence of how the name expanded across the settlements.

II. The Story of Eleuthera

The Eleutherian Adventurers were a sect of seventy migrants from Great Britain and Bermuda who were promised land to cultivate in return for their loyalty to their country. They were also promised religious freedom. The island of destination was Cigatoo (Eleuthera), which had been mostly uninhabited for 150 years (but for unsuccessful attempts). Cigatoo was derived from the Arawak Indians' original name for the island.[38]

The settlers took refuge at Preacher's Cave, where sermons were delivered. Elderly Reverend Copeland, age 78, arrived with the group and became their religious leader.[39]

---

[36] Bahamas Civil Registration, Department of Archives, www.familysearch.org.

[37] Registrar General's Department, Documents, Eleuthera 1850–90, www.familysearch.org.

[38] Paul Albury, *The Story of the Bahamas* (St Martin's Press, 1976).

[39] Sir John Henry Lefroy, *Memorials of the Discovery and Early Settlement of the Bermudas or Somers Islands,* vol. II, 78.

The 1670 census, which is closer timewise to the 1720 census, details surnames such as Albury, Bethel, Bullard, Butler, Cartwright, Culmer, Knowles, Nottage, Pinder, Sands, Russell, Thompson, and Williams. Historical 1720 land grants show land granted to brothers William, Richard, and James Culmer from their king, as well as other settlers.[40] However, it is also recorded throughout history that grants were given in 1670 to the Lord Proprietors of Virginia, with England retaining full rights by 1717. Furthermore, many records on the island were lost in the hurricane of 1829. However, many people with the same surnames remained settled in the same parts of the island.

The settlers of Eleuthera enjoyed a less structured society than their Nassauvian counterparts, who had brought the customs and cultures of the loyalist society with them from the southern states after the US War of Independence.[41] The expedition to Eleuthera was used as an example not to be repeated. However, it was alleged that once they arrived, the inhabitants of New Providence were enjoying a long life of one hundred years and older, surrendering mostly to fatigue.[42]

Eleuthera had a different background, in that the settlers were more experienced and were descendants of original settlers.[43] Also, the Eleutherans were not keen on

---

[40] Department of Lands and Surveys, Nassau.

[41] Craton, *A History of the Bahamas.*

[42] Ibid., Lefroy, 265.

[43] Albury, *The Story of the Bahamas.*

the systematic structures of these new families and the instilling of new registration requirements.[44]

A 1734 census also records the original Sands men, Peter Sr and a son, Peter Jr. There were also Samuel and John and their families. By that time, William and Richard Thompson, as well as the European Russell families, lived on the island. Moreover, the locals were in scattered settlements along Eleuthera, living a settled life on produce and the salt industry. The Foreign and Commonwealth office also visited, and notes described life on the island for settlers.[45] It would be some decades for the island to evolve with the introduction of different industries, education, and newer settlers from the British Isles and the rest of the world.

Central Eleuthera

[44] Ibid.
[45] Department of Archives, FCO notes.

Public record notes that one Richard Culmer, born by 1740, died in the early 1800s.[46] There were several alive between 1766 and the 1880s in Tarpum Bay (which was said to be started by the Culmer and Carey families from Ireland).[47] They were the patriarchs of their families and had originated from the United Kingdom and followed generations of all walks of life using the same name.[48] Another Richard, who lived in Savannah Sound, had married a Susannah Carey[49] but would have been born too close in time to our Richard Culmer of Glenelg, born in 1843, to be his parent.

Richard Culmer Sr (or II) of Glenelg, a European listed farmer, was born in 1843, place unknown, and died in the 1920s[50] on Eleuthera. He was born after the Abolition in the British territories. As evidenced in his will, he had six children and one surviving wife. He was the great-great-grandfather of this book's author. It is still not certain precisely how this surname expanded among so many settlements during the latter part of the nineteenth century.

Richard Sr was a local landowner. There were other Richards of his age living on Eleuthera, as stated above, with different death dates, as well as offspring he would

---

[46] Place of birth unknown.

[47] www.eleuthera.com, www.familysearch.org.

[48] Civil Registration, Bahamas, deaths, 1850–90.

[49] Bahamas Birth records, Eleuthera, Department of Archives.

[50] Registrar General's Department, Nassau, Birth and Death records, Eleuthera.

produce, with two more direct Richard descendants in his lifetime.

A map of Savannah Sound from the 1890s shows the households living in the township, including Bullard, Culmer, Thompson, Sands Sr, Clarke Sr, and another pre-existing Sands family of the local David, as well as commonage land now settled, and the Ministry of Education building, which was a schoolhouse.

Richard Culmer Sr of Glenelg was also closely associated with Deal Clarke Sr, who died in 1899[51] and was also listed in 1903. Deal was born in the early 1820s and is presumed to be connected to the Irish George Clarke,[52] who married Eliza Sands and arrived at the town in the 1820s.

One George Clarke was born in the early 1800s and died in the late 1880s.[53] Their son, George Alexander Clarke, was born in the 1850s. Deal Clarke also purchased acreage in the district of Glenelg starting in the mid-1800s. He had married Diannah Sands from the local family of New Portsmouth.[54] His first son was Deal Clarke Jr, born in the early 1850s. There was a popular former settlement called Deal's Point in the 1840s, now defunct, which suggests the surname was also on the island. Eleutheran villagers in the 1890s had migrated to the Keys and Dade County, where they were farmers or were drafted in World War I.

[51] Eleuthera Marriage, Birth and Death Index pre-1900.
[52] Bahamas DNA Project, http://genealogy.hopetownmuseum.com.
[53] Civil Registration, Bahamas, deaths, www.familysearch.org.
[54] Civil Registration, Bahamas, deaths, 1907, www.familysearch.org.

Recorded as drafted, but uncertified whether he served was Samuel Alonzo Sands of Florida,[55] born in the late 1870s. He had an uncle in Eleuthera, William Henry Sands, who died circa 1895[56] and had married Eliza Knowles. Samuel Alonzo, who married Laura, originally from Eleuthera and the United Kingdom, had brothers. Alexander Jr was born in the 1870s and another William Henry Jr was born in 1867; he was the former Commissioner of Eleuthera.[57] He is not to be confused with the one from Tarpum Bay, who died the same year on a different day. The aforesaid's second wife was a Vera Carey.[58] This William Henry Jr also had a sister, Mary Ann Kates. These were the children of Alexander Sr with his former wife, Matilda. Several Alexander Sands are recorded in the nineteenth century; however, it is unknown how directly or specifically related they are to the previously mentioned.

It has been formerly stated that the missionary Sands family arrived or resettled in the 1840s (a father, Alexander, arrived with two young sons, William and Alexander)[59] and later moved to eastern Savannah Sound. Alexander Sr (d. ca. 1903)[60] married Matilda (d. ca. 1885),[61] from a then well-known family. It has been stated by earlier

---

[55] US Draft WWI records.

[56] Department of Archives, Nassau.

[57] Registrar General's Department, Nassau, births.

[58] Bahamas Marriage Records, Zion Baptist Church, Rev. Talmadge Sands.

[59] Oral account from family members.

[60] No record of death in the Bahamas.

[61] www.familysearch.org.

relatives that they were from the British Isles, referred to by my ancestors and elders as the "old country." Certain documents are not present in Eleuthera. This particular Sands family settled later. Eleuthera, as well as other islands, where another affluent William Henry Sands[62] lived in the 1890s, had become a Sands settlement with the initial Sands family living in Rock Sound or New Portsmouth, with relatives by this point all over the island and moving to the states.

It was a fact that the island provided a refuge for people who were escaping famine or poverty around the world, since it was still British territory. During Victorian times, the islands were attractive to those who needed a new life or were propelled by some humanitarian cause. These families farmed tomatoes and pineapples (which were large industries), had creeks which contained salt, and fished and were involved in the sponging industry. My father, G. Clifford Culmer, still remembers the Culmer family salt mine.

It was noted that other Sands families from New Portsmouth were marine men, such as James Alexander, who sailed aboard *The Catherine*,[63] named after his mother, in the 1890s. Another renowned set settled in Palmetto Point from the original line who owned businesses in that community.

Other settlers in the community consisted of Sawyer, Thompson, Rankine, Gibson, and later, the McCartney family of Tarpum Bay. The latter's paternal migrants also arrived in the mid-1850s from the British Isles and listed

---

[62] Department of Archives, Nassau.
[63] 1800 ships online registry documents.

their offspring legally in documents. In addition, the records show a distinct population boom at that time.[64] By 1904, Alexander Sands Sr (Or II) of Savannah Sound, who was born abroad in the 1830s, the relative of missionaries, had passed and left about fourteen surviving children from Eleuthera, which was then still British territory. Some of these children migrated or travelled to and from the Keys, where he is presumed and noted to have married his second wife, Rebecca, in the late 1880s, with the priest as a witness.[65] Their last son was the Reverend Talmage Sands (MBE[66]). However, his youngest daughter, Sarah, was a toddler when he died and looked strikingly similar to her older sisters, Rophelia (who married an Austrian WWI veteran, and was matriarch of a respected New Jersey family) and Nelly Marie, who married into an affluent family in Boston and was born in the 1890s.[67]

The new century showed a significant change for Eleuthera. The children of these nineteenth-century landowners owned land in family groups and established a homogeneous social status. Many families like theirs devised property to all their children and grandchildren before the 1970s.

---

[64] Department of Archives, Nassau.

[65] Jesus Christ Church of Latter Day Saints NYC. Munroe County, Key West records 1880–90.

[66] Member of the British Empire awarded.

[67] Registrar General's Department, Department of Archives, Nassau.

Playground by the Ancestral Bay in the
1970s. Culmer family collection

Wesleyan Methodist Church.
Copyright Gabrielle F. Culmer

Church at Tarpum Bay. Copyright Gabrielle F. Culmer

CHAPTER 4

Nassau

Many families migrated to Nassau and the United States. The district of Glenelg Sands and Culmer families, as well as others, migrated to Nassau and Florida and helped form these societies in Coconut Grove and beyond, including Hallandale. One, the late Edith Culmer, a centenarian, arrived with her American niece, Sarah Claretta, from Eleuthera. Great-Aunt Cora had also moved for a period, while cousin Harrold moved and was our stand-in tour guide on holiday. The descendants of Eleuthera's first settlers had earlier moved to Nassau to form commercial townships and affluent residential areas.

There is also another line which produced Sir Stafford Sands, the former Finance Minister, the aforesaid William H. Sands (d. 1800s), and other notable names. From Eleuthera and Savannah Sound came the composer of the national anthem. Also, the renowned Reverend Talmage Sands MBE (d. 1983), who was the grand-uncle of the author and stood in as grandfather, was recognized as one of the most notable men of the twentieth century for his religious leadership and charitable works. He was the last child of Alexander. Talmage resembled his father's first sons with Matilda, who were born before she died. Talmage became the patriarch of the extended family and would even visit his siblings in Florida and Boston to provide moral and small charitable support.

The later influx of Eleutherans to Nassau occurred in the 1950s when a new set of young professionals would eventually form the country in the areas of business, medicine, and law. One was my father, G. Clifford, who had won a scholarship to Nassau after his biological mother, Sarah, born in the early 1900s[68] and the youngest daughter of the late Alexander Sr, had passed. She was known in the settlement and the country for her beauty and silky hair to her waistline. Clifford was sent to live with his uncle Talmage and wife, Dora, in Nassau to finish high school. He then continued his accounting training in England with their children and his first cousins Hugh (CMG, Companion of the Order of St Michael and St. George), an educator and banker, James,[69] Sydney, and Clarice (OBE),[70] wife of the late Dean, William Granger.

G. Clifford is the youngest son of Arthur Culmer (b. 1890s)[71] and half-Scottish Sarah Carolina. Arthur was also the grandson of the local Diannah (née Sands) and Deal Clarke Sr and was the second son of Richard Jr and his first wife. Arthur and his siblings were farmers and landowners. G. Clifford is named after the former king and the governor

---

[68] Registrar General's Department, Nassau.

[69] Wives are June, Emerald, and Shantee.

[70] Order of the British Empire.

[71] Ibid. Births and Deaths, Nassau.

of the formerly named Bahama Islands. His family wanted him in an office profession, a dream culminating from three hundred years of Eleutheran farming settlers. He married upon returning from England, Corliss, who was from a well-educated veteran (UK) and well-known Nassuvian family.

These aforesaid individuals became a modern established family from the community. The other siblings were dispersed among Nassau, Florida, and Eleuthera and set up businesses in Nassau and Eleuthera. Included is a locally skilled baker, Cora Leone, who married Henry, the local Justice of the Peace, baker, and pastor. Another business owner, Eliza Eileen, married a McCartney (CBE)[72] of Tarpum Bay. The wife of the late ambassador to the UN (L.B., CBE), Charmian, was raised by Arthur and his second wife, Rev. Carmetta. Leonard (deceased), from Florida, was one Culmer brother who fought in World War II, and another, Wardell (a former warden, deceased), worked on Windermere Island, where a young Clifford would watch his father farm on his grandmother's land.

Included in this set of popular Eleutherans was the first Premier, as stated, the composer of the Bahamas' national anthem, as well as many educators.

By the 1980s most of Eleuthera had running water and electricity and was visited by famous people. Many international notable resorts were highly depended on for work to subsidize the communities. Still today, the economy depends on tourism, fishing, and imports. The success of its people can also be seen in other structured communities as well as building a nation at home.

---

[72] William Alfred, Commander of the British Empire.

Photo of The Author at the Ancestral Bay.
Copyright Gabrielle F. Culmer

CONCLUSION

A long history has been detailed beginning from AD 792 and the period after the War of the Roses to modern-day Southern American and Eleutheran societies. The resilience of these people is to be admired, and the contributions they have made to society throughout the centuries are immeasurable. The population boom in the 1850s added greater opportunity in the years to come. The Sands family were initially larger and visionary and expanded further with many variations. They are also very generous.

The Culmer family and families like theirs, although smaller, had more control of their lineage through documentation until the twentieth century. Eleuthera thrived in the twentieth century through development, tourism, and migration.

Undoubtedly, new information is arising yearly, which may dispute some of this information later; however, reliable records were used at the time of the writing to come to the aforesaid conclusions. Some dates and names have been altered for privacy. Also, research was numerically and statistically based, and the author wishes to refrain from personal comments about the livelihoods of any ancestors and named individuals.

BIBLIOGRAPHY

Albury, P., *The Story of the Bahamas*, St Martin's Press (1976).

Archbold, WAJ, "William Sandys, Baron Sandys of the Vine", in *The Dictionary of National Biography*.

Baker, O., *History of the Antiquities of Sandwich and Richborough Castle in Kent*, 86.

Craton, M., *A History of the Bahamas* (3rd edn, 2nd printing, San Salvador Press, 1987), 54–9.

Craton, M. and G. Saunders, *Islanders in the Stream: A History of the Bahamian People*, vol. 2 (2000).

Department of Archives, Mackey Street, Nassau.

Fritze, R., "Sandys, William, First Baron Sandys", in *Oxford Dictionary of National Biography*, vol. XVII (New York: Macmillan, 1909), 785.

Lefroy, Sir John Henry, *Memorials of the Discovery and Early Settlement of the Bermudas or Somers Islands,* vol. II, 1650–1687.

Lefroy, Robert, *Memorials of the Early Settlement of Bermuda*, vol. II. In Proceedings of the Massachusetts Historical Society.

Luminarium: Encyclopedia project.

Northbourne Sources: Tudor Place

Pleasants, H., *The Lovelace Family and Its Connections: Sandys of Furnace Fells, Lancashire.* The Virginia Magazine of History and Biography, vol. 27.

(Longmans, Green and Co., 1877). www.archive.org.

The Registers of the Parish of St John, Thanet, Kent. October 1559–March 1635.

Registrar General's Department, Nassau.

Reynolds Historical Genealogy Collection.

A Rootsweb: Bahamas/1999–2010/0939061009.

Who's Who of Tudor Women. (2014 reviewed.)

www.ancestry.com: Lookups in early ancestry.

www.archive.org: Full Text of Virginia county records, 975.5 V6 pt. 1 (1909).

www.archive.org: Full Text of the Knights of England.

www.cumbria-wildlife.org.uk.

www.FamilySearch.org: Civil Registration.

www.familysearch.org: Culmer Genealogy from 862 to 1913.

www.houseofnames.com: Culmer family crest and history.

www.sandsancestry.net.

Printed in the United States
By Bookmasters